CW01080700

BOOK ANALYSIS

By Joanna Glum

Lincoln in the Bardo
by George Saunders

Bright
≡Summaries.com

GEORGE SAUNDERS

AMERICAN WRITER

- **Born in Amarillo, Texas in 1958.**
- **Notable works:**
  - *CivilWarLand in Bad Decline* (1996), short story collection
  - *Pastoralia* (2000), short story collection
  - *Tenth of December* (2013) short story collection

George Saunders is an American author, renowned for his work with the short story form. Having studied under the writer Tobias Wolff whilst earning his M.A. in Creative Writing at Syracuse University, Saunders went on to write technical manuals for seven years before publishing his first short story collection in 1996. From 1997, Saunders has served as lecturer in Creative Writing at Syracuse University; in 2006 he was awarded both the Guggenheim and MacArthur Fellowships. A frequent contributor to publications like the *New Yorker* and *McSweeney's*, Saunders has won the PEN/Malamud Award, the Folio Prize, and the Man Booker Prize in the course of his career.

LINCOLN IN THE BARDO

LYRICAL, SPECULATIVE FICTION

- **Genre:** novel (experimental, tragicomic)
- **Reference edition:** Saunders, G. (2017) *Lincoln in the Bardo*. London: Bloomsbury.
- **1st edition:** 2017
- **Themes:** regret, metaphysics and spirituality, mortality and the afterlife, importance and ineffectuality, empathy and human connectivity

Lincoln in the Bardo details the night in 1862 that Abraham Lincoln spent in the graveyard where he had earlier buried his young son, Willie. However, the majority of the book's action takes place in a spirit world, where the dead refuse to accept that they are dead, instead believing themselves sick, to avoid 'passing on'. Blurring the line between the world of the living and the world of the dead, *Lincoln in the Bardo* blends fiction and history, alternating between the voices of the fictional characters in the graveyard and both factual and quasi-factual historical references.

Winner of the Man Booker Prize in 2017 and Saunders' first novel, *Lincoln in the Bardo* is a meditation on what it is to have a meaningful life. As spirits cling to their spirit world, hoping one day to return to their former lives in order to make amends or experience that which they were previously unable to, Lincoln wrestles with the decision to leave his precious son to resume his duties as President of a United States torn apart by the Civil War. In all, Saunders explores the ways in which we define ourselves, the ways in which we reduce others in our perceptions of them, and how true liberation comes from understanding and empathising with strangers.

SUMMARY

PART 1: WILLIE LINCOLN DIES AND ENTERS THE BARDO

The novel opens with Hans Vollman discussing his marriage to his much younger wife, and how they had decided to remain friends until they developed such a strong bond that she wished to consummate the marriage. Before they could, however, a beam struck Vollman and sent him to a "sick-box" (p. 5), which clearly means his coffin. He and his friend, Roger Bevins III, comment on how young the new arrival to the "hospital-yard" (p. 8) is.

Saunders then quotes historical sources which recount the events of a state dinner that the Lincolns held one winter during the Civil War, which offended many with its lavishness – and during which the Lincolns' son Willie was morbidly ill with fever. The guests at the party describe the lavishness of the display and provide contradictory accounts of the moon the evening of the party. An account from Isabelle Perkins' Civil War letters reveals that Willie had died and Lincoln had placed him in a crypt belonging to Judge Carroll opposite the Perkins' home.

In the graveyard, Roger Bevins III recounts how he slit his wrists after his lover broke up with him in order to repress his homosexual tendencies. However, as he began to die, Bevins changed his mind, and he says that he is waiting to be revived in his former kitchen. Vollman halts Bevins' reverie, careful not to scare the new arrival – the dead Willie Lincoln. Willie remarks that Bevins has multiple sets of eyes, hands, and noses and that Vollman is nude with an exceptionally large erection – the exaggerated features of that which the characters had hoped to use more of in life. They are joined by the Reverend Thomas, whose hair shoots straight up and whose mouth forms, "a perfect O of terror" (p. 28). Though the others suggest Willie might to go somewhere else – a euphemism for his spirit passing into death – Willie tells them that he must wait for his parents. However, the men say that the young must not and often do not stay around for long, so they take Willie to "the edge of an uninhabited wilderness...that ended in the dreaded iron fence" (p. 36).

There they find Elsie Traynor, a young girl whose spirit has not passed on as it should have. She transforms into a number of unpleasant things. She softens for Willie, however, and tells him how she died at 14, desired to have a child, and learned vulgar words in death that she did not know in life. Willie seems convinced that he must pass on, but as soon as the men lead him back to his crypt, Willie spots his father. Though he tries to embrace Lincoln, his ghost passes through him, and Lincoln moves to Willie's crypt and removes his body.

Historical accounts detail Willie's fatal decline and Lincoln's heartbroken, sobbing response to having lost his favourite son. They detail how beloved Willie was by everybody for being an intelligent, thoughtful boy and how ravaged with grief the Lincolns were at his death. At the graveyard, a crowd has gathered to watch Lincoln holding Willie's exhumed corpse. Willie, frustrated that his father is not paying attention to him, enters his body as Lincoln holds it. However, he also partially enters Lincoln's body and begins to hear his father's thoughts and his promise to return to Willie in order to gain some strength of spirit.

Lincoln leaves, and Willie tells the Reverend that his father promised to return. Having seen a living person love one of the dead, even going so far as to touch them, the other spirits in the graveyard emerge and enjoy each other's company.

They soon line up to talk to Willie in hopes that he might return to the land of the living. The spirits recount their lives: Jane Ellis asks Willie to reassure her daughters in her absence, Abigail Blass offers all of the money and debris she has saved, and Lieutenant Cecil Strong recounts with racist epithets his former life as a slave-owner. More arrive to speak with Willie, but cannot because the graveyard blossoms with foliage and natural life as it is invaded by spirits that take the form of the seers' object of desire in life (angels for the Reverend, brides for Vollman, his lover for Bevins). These apparitions attempt to lure the graveyard's inhabitants to leave with them – ostensibly passing on into whatever lies beyond their purgatory.

Given the promise of a pill that can give her all she ever lacked in life, Mrs. Abigail Blass leaves with her visions with a shout and "the matterlightblooming phenomenon" (p. 96). The apparitions try to lure all with them with more vigour, making the spirits confront the fact that they are dead and must pass on. However, they eventually leave and the graveyard returns to its grey state. Bevins, Vollman, and the Reverend try to ascertain who were the three spirits taken, and although they assume Willie is one, they find him still in the graveyard though in a deteriorated state.

A tendril grows and attaches itself to Willie, and the three men lament that if he stays he will become a part of the crypt, as Elsie Traynor had become part of the gate, doomed to an existence without much hope or aspiration. Willie resolves to remain, and the men note that Jane Ellis was the third to have passed on. Then, they are bombarded with hate and practical jokes from the three bachelors – rabble-rousers who can fly and have remained "in a youthful state of perpetual emotional vacuity" (p. 118). They say they saw Lincoln not long ago and then leave. The Reverend tells Bevins and Vollman that they must not tell Willie for Willie's sake. The Reverend disappears, but Bevins and Vollman choose to investigate out of boredom with their situation.

They encounter Trevor Williams, a former hunter who, in the graveyard, became burdened by those animals he killed in life, fated to hold hundreds of them until they felt ready to pass on. They pass Percival "Dash" Collier, who, having had many properties in life, now finds his head turned into a compass, pointing for eternity towards whichever property he was most concerned with at the moment. Bevins and Vollman cross the swamp, where the residents have become shapeless, formless grey lines, and move beyond to the most freshly-dug "sick-hole" (p. 136) of Tober Muller.

From that place, Captain William Prince, a former soldier, attempts to write to his wife. Discovering that he is in a graveyard, he confesses to his wife that he had been carrying on an affair in life. As he confesses, he disappears with the same "matterlightblooming phenomenon" (p. 140). Other spirits perform crude gestures on the man's grave. Bevins and Vollman move on, past the markers of those whose spirits did not linger in the graveyard. Bevins and Vollman criticise them for having "surrendered" (p. 144). They finally encounter Lincoln.

Bevins and Vollman occupy Lincoln's body and are able to understand his thought process. Influenced by the younger Bevins, Lincoln remembers an image of a girl from his youth, grows ashamed, and tries to redirect his attention to remembering Willy in life, but he cannot. He finally recalls how delighted Willy was when he was fitted for the suit in which he is now buried. Lincoln mourns his son, but his thoughts digress. Historical testimony recounts the bodies of dead soldiers in the bloody battles of the Civil War.

Lincoln goes on to think about how thousands have lost their sons, and he tells himself he must not capitulate and must push forward with the war. He thinks about Willie being in a better place, but Vollman and Bevins discuss with one another how sad it is that Willie is, in fact, not in a better place. The two resolve to attempt to influence Lincoln to return to Willie's tomb and to persuade him to assure Willie that he will not be returning – this in the hopes that Willie might then pass on.

Bevins and Vollman indicate that they have previously managed to have sway over the living, as once they convinced a fighting couple to reconcile to the point that they were able to watch the couple make love in the graveyard. After trying numerous tactics, the two begin to think about the horror of an unlocked tomb, prompting Lincoln to recall that he had not locked Willie's tomb after leaving. Lincoln leaves to go to the tomb, Bevins and Vollman having been successful.

On the way back, Bevins and Vollman inhabit each other inadvertently and are able to envision one another's former lives, which they find "intensely pleasurable" (p. 172). They lose Lincoln in the process, and disengage from one another to pursue him. They find they have a more intrinsic understanding not only of one another, but of Lincoln as well. They find that they know that Lincoln is the President, among other details about contemporary technology and fashion. They speed to Willie's tomb.

PART 2: LINCOLN MUST DECIDE TO LEAVE THE GRAVEYARD AND MARCH INTO THE FUTURE

Historical accounts indicate that those at the White House wondered whether Lincoln would be able to competently lead the country again after the crisis. They say that Mary Lincoln had gone hysterical with Willie's death and needed to be heavily sedated for nearly a month afterwards. Meanwhile, the Reverend attempts to persuade Willie to leave, saying that that place is not a very healthy environment. Willie retorts by asking why the Reverend chooses to stay, and the Reverend explains that, unlike the others, he is aware that he is dead.

In an extended passage, the Reverend describes how, when he was buried, he passed on and with two companions marched to a hall of judgement wherein sat a ledger. Though he initially passed back to the graveyard, where he was aware of having been buried, he saw his two companions face judgment in the afterlife. After having their minds read by two beings there and their hearts weighted on a scale, and being forced to face themselves in the mirror, one was led to a hall of indescribable splendour, the other damned to a hall full of flayed human bodies. When the Reverend was in line to be judged, those in the hall indicated that he had failed, and, assuming he would therefore meet horrible damnation, the Reverend returned to the graveyard, forbidden from revealing the truth of the judgement in afterlife to anyone. He stays in order to hide from damnation despite knowing that, as he is dead, there is nothing he can do to change his situation in the afterlife. His reverie ends when Bevins and Vollman return, rejoicing at having convinced Lincoln to return with the lock. The Reverend is struck by Lincoln's face, and historical accounts describe how Lincoln had sad eyes, though animated when happy, and how he was universally regarded as ugly. However, in spite of this, the accounts say that his sense of kindness and generosity was most evident in his face and made him lovely to look on.

At the tomb, Lincoln is unable to resist looking at Willie's body once more, and Vollman frees Willie from the roof, where he had grown trapped by the growing tendrils, so that the boy may inhabit his father's body to hear Lincoln's thoughts. Meanwhile, a growing crowd has formed, and they begin to shout out confessions about everything: having stolen, having been molested, having always thought themselves dumb, or having always thought themselves unrecognised for their earthly accomplishments. Many of them protest as the spirits of slaves begin to approach the tomb.

Elson Farwell, a friend of the Barons, is the first to speak, and his speech is so elevated that the Barons cannot understand him. He describes how he had been promoted as a slave to a house slave, but that, walking one day in the summer heat with the children of whom he took care, he collapsed and was forgotten. In his dying moments, he fantasised about regaining strength to fight his slave-owners to regain "a certain modicum of humanity" (p. 217). Thomas Havens, another slave, commented that while he attempted to make the best of his life, the moments that he continues to think about are those moments he had completely to himself, and it bothers him to think that some people have entire lives as such.

Another young slave, Lizzie Wright, is unable to speak. Mrs. Francis Hodges, whose feet and hands are now just bloody stumps, tells the others that Lizzie does not speak because in life she was used and abused by men and had been forced to comply. Lieutenant Stone leads an army of red-faced white men to chase the slaves away, and the two groups reach a standoff at the border gate, where the slaves do not experience its noxious effects and so hold their ground.

Meanwhile, Manders the groundskeeper interrupts at the moment that Willie is going to enter Lincoln. As Lincoln leaves, the tendrils growing from the tomb grab Willie once more and entrap him worse than before. While Bevins tries to free Willie, Vollman enters Lincoln to attempt to persuade him to remain. Lincoln is thinking about how to formulate a positive goodbye, though it is hard for him to be positive, especially in light of the fact that he is currently disliked in the country. Historical accounts give the opinions of those who found Lincoln incompetent and to blame for the as-yet disastrous and seemingly pointless continued Civil War. They also articulate the racist sentiments of those who did not wish to fight on behalf of African-Americans.

Though Lincoln tries to soothe himself by saying that no one in history has ever gone without criticism, and that at least with Willie he cannot be criticised, historical accounts blame Lincoln for not having been a better parent, having let Willie ride his pony in the cold, implying that it was for this reason that he took ill. They continue that, though Mrs. Lincoln wanted to cancel all social engagements, Lincoln urged her not to and summoned a doctor who said that Willie would recover, and having trusted the doctor, Lincoln let their party continue on the day of Willie's death.

Vollman, still within Lincoln, hears him trying to animate Willie's lifeless body in his head, though Lincoln says he is being superstitious. Though Vollman tries to persuade Lincoln to stay, Lincoln closes the tomb and leaves just as Bevins frees Willie. The two resolve to band together to inhabit Lincoln's body, and though the Reverend vowed not to do so again after discovering that the couple they had reconciled had been ruined with the wife's suicide, he joins the other two. All of the spirits in the graveyard eventually join in, except for Stone, who refuses to follow given that the spirits of slaves have also entered Lincoln. Together in Lincoln and so comforted by their unified, communal spirit, all begin to recall moments of solidarity with their community in life. Remembering this, they feel "restored somewhat to [their] natural fullness" (p. 256). The gross exaggerations in their bodies or expressions disappear (e.g. Bevins' multitude of eyes and noses), and all appear not just as they were in life, but as they were in the prime of their life. Nonetheless, Lincoln does not return to the tomb.

The three petition the Bachelors for their help, but unwilling to do anything that is not of their own accord, the Bachelors decline and send down funereal bowler hats. The group grows discouraged, and all eventually leave Lincoln's body. Vollman, Bevins, and the Reverend, after trying to recall without success the reasons why he was damned, return to the tomb to help Willie. They find he is encrusted by a carapace and assume he will pass on. However, voices from the tomb, those of great sinners, offer to take Willie to the roof for the rest of eternity. The Reverend pleads for mercy for Willie because he had never sinned as they had, but the voices of the demons say that they had no choice to be other than what they were – a paedophile, a misanthrope who killed her husband, a couple who killed their baby to spare him from a life of misery. The Reverend asks them to release Willie to the roof, but he steals Willie and runs off before they can take him.

The demons, though, chase after the Reverend and overtake him, trapping both him and Willie in a carapace. Bevins and Vollman chase after, but the Reverend decides to let go, and there is another matterlightblooming phenomenon. Bevins and Vollman manage to free Willie from the carapace, and, attempting to finish the Reverend's mission, run Willie in turns to the chapel in an attempt to escape the demons. When they manage to enter the chapel, though, the demons follow. However, they are interrupted as they see Lincoln sitting in a pew. Other spirits begin to enter the chapel, and Bevins and Vollman encourage Willie to enter Lincoln. He does, and he hears his father recalling their last moment together before Willie took ill.

Historical accounts detail how Willie's fever developed into typhoid and how his father, naturally an empathetic man, was wracked with grief watching Willie succumb to the violent symptoms of the disease. Vollman orders Willie to come out of his father, seeing how his father's thoughts are troubling him. Historical accounts go on to describe Willie's embalming process with zinc chloride, and Bevins notices that Willie has grown still inside his father. The accounts continue, detailing the events of Willie's funeral, with the final account saying that Lincoln left the chapel saying, "Willie is dead...as if it had just occurred to him" (p. 294).

Willie stands and exits his father. He joyfully proclaims to all that they are not sick but are indeed dead. He says that they must all pass on as they should, for they could never return to that other place no matter how nice it was. Though Vollman protests, Bevins considers that perhaps Willie has a point. Spirits around begin to falter with Willie's repeated proclamation that they are dead, and, eventually, Willie himself goes with a matterlightblooming phenomenon after briefly taking many of his previous physical forms and his future forms (as newlywed, husband, widower, old man). As soon as Willie disappears, Lincoln stands and leaves rapidly, passing through Bevins and Vollman, who can hear Lincoln reaffirm that his son is dead and will never return.

They continue to hear Lincoln consider how his suffering is not unique and that all of humanity is connected by a common experience of suffering and of loss. While he feels humility and overwhelming empathy, he continues to think that he must endeavour to continue the Civil War with maximum efficiency in order to "end suffering by causing more suffering" (p. 307). Though Lincoln is conflicted about continuing the war, in recalling how he was able to rise from poverty and anonymity to a place where he might be able to grant the right to pursue that kind of life and happiness for *all* people, he ultimately concludes that he must continue to fight for this right.

Exiting, Lincoln passes through Francis Hodge who is glad to hear Lincoln's resolve to continue the war. Thomas Havens stays inside Lincoln for a while, and he endeavours to share with Lincoln his personal history, Lizzie's, Francis', and Elson's history, as well as the history of every other slave he had known in the hope that it might inspire Lincoln to liberate them. Lizzie returns with the news that they are dead, and she and Francis Hodge leave, while Elson defiantly stays. Lincoln rides away from the graveyard, and Manders and Perkins, the invalid girl across the way, exchange a goodnight.

As the spirits begin to leave, Lieutenant Stone has an angry outburst against Mr. Farwell, ordering him back to work, and the two men engage in a confrontation that continues to go on, with Bevins suspecting it might continue indefinitely "unless some fundamental and unimaginable alteration of reality should occur" (p. 321). Bevins and Vollman watch as the Barons eventually succumb to the matterlightblooming phenomenon, and Bevins begins to waver.

He recalls that on the day of his suicide he saw his lover in public with another man, despite having been told that he was going to live a heteronormative life. He asks Vollman to remember how his wife had visited a year ago to thank him for preparing her to accept her future husband, the great love of her life. Vollman begins to weep, and he and Bevins resolve to leave together. Vollman watches as Bevins assumes his future form as a content lover with his partner. However, the two do not leave yet as they remember the Traynor girl. They head to her to apologise for having convinced her to stay when she first arrived, and they ask her to leave now, but she refuses.

Vollman resolves to step inside the form she has taken at the moment – that of a burning railcar – and in doing so assumes his future forms as contented husband and grandfather. Inside the burning car, Traynor asks Vollman to blow up the railcar in the hope that it might free her; with the matterlightblooming phenomenon, the railcar explodes and both Traynor and Vollman disappear. Bevins, taking a last inventory of all of the beautiful things in life, says goodbye and also disappears.

The remaining spirits who did not succumb, including the Bachelors, enter their bodies before daylight breaks; though they hate the smell, they suffer through it in order to live again during the night. Manders closes up Willie's tomb, thinking about his own son and how he neither wishes to experience the pain of losing a child nor make them endure their own deaths without him there to help. He hopes his friend, Tom, will arrive soon to relieve him of his duties.

Thomas Haven rides on, still inside Lincoln, hearing how the President is chastising himself for having left his wife and his other son, Tad. Lincoln again resolves to carry on and to be strong for all, and Haven endeavours to stay there as they ride back to the White House.

CHARACTER STUDY

HANS VOLLMAN

Hans Vollman, along with Roger Bevins III and the Reverend Everly Thomas, makes up the trio of figures who usher both Willie and the reader through the world of the Bardo. In life, Vollman had lived a modest life as a print-maker, and though he took pride in his work, he was ultimately lonely until he was married to a much younger, beautiful wife. The two did not consummate their marriage, given her timidity and his respect for her wishes, and lived instead like brother and sister. However, with their deepened connection, Vollman's wife asked him to finally consummate their marriage, but on the day they were to do so, Vollman had a heart attack and died. As a result, his exaggerated physical aspect in the Bardo is an enormous erection. He risks his own safety to help Willie pass over, and though he is the last of the trio to accept that he is dead, he passes over in order to free the young Traynor girl from her eternal imprisonment.

ROGER BEVINS III

Bevins is part of the trio of characters that guides the story. He arrived in the Bardo after committing suicide, having done so after seeing his male lover with another man; however, he stays in the Bardo thinking that his suicide attempt has failed and that he needs merely to recover. Prone to extended poetic passages detailing little, but poignantly observing life's day-to-day-beauty, Bevins has multiple eyes, ears, noses, and hands in the Bardo and grows more with each reminiscence of life's sensory pleasures. He is the final of the trio to pass on and continually risks himself in order to help Willie pass on.

THE REVEREND EVERLY THOMAS

The elder of the trio of main characters, the Reverend remarks that he is different because, rather than believing he is merely sick and his coffin merely a sick-bed, he knows that he is dead. Having first arrived in the Bardo, he passed on, but upon seeing the horror of damnation on the other side, and having been judged to be damned on his initial passing, the Reverend ran back to the Bardo so as to avoid his punishment. As a result, his mouth in the Bardo makes a perfect O, and his hair stands straight up.

The Reverend continually attempts to figure out what it was he had done in a former life to condemn him, but to no avail. After hearing the voices of the demons that trap Willie in a carapace – those of former sinners – he resolves that he cannot be judged in the same way as them. The Reverend is the first to save Willie from a fate of being trapped in the Bardo, running him to the chapel, and he is the first to pass on in order to help Willie.

WILLIE LINCOLN

Seen by both the characters in the Bardo and the historical accounts included throughout the book, Willie is a perfect young boy, "the sort of child people imagine their children will be, before they have children" (p. 51). He arrives in the Bardo after dying of typhoid fever, and when his father visits his tomb, Willie is reluctant to leave, believing that Lincoln will return to collect him. Being young, Willie succumbs quickly to the entrapments of the Bardo which would preclude him from passing on and keep him possessed by demons and misery. He is brought to the chapel by the Reverend, Bevins, and Vollman, who encourage Willie to inhabit Lincoln's body. When Willie learns that he is dead, he rejoices and tells all in the Bardo, precipitating the passing of a majority of the spirits. Once Willie passes on, his father feels able to leave the Bardo, and both reconcile their feelings of grief with the knowledge they must move on.

ABRAHAM LINCOLN

Abraham Lincoln is the President of the United States of America and, at the time of the events in the book, he is leading the Union in the middle of a seemingly fruitless Civil War. He returns to his son's tomb the night following the funeral and takes him from the coffin to hold him once more; overcome by grief at Willie's loss, Lincoln has a hard time leaving the graveyard and eventually rests to pray in the chapel on the grounds. Once Willie passes on from the Bardo, Lincoln resolves not to wallow in grief but to return to his wife, his other son, and his position at the head of the country.

Throughout, Lincoln is preoccupied with both Willie's death and the shadow of the Civil War. Historical accounts provide contradictory perceptions of Lincoln, with some blaming his negligence for Wille's death and others condemning the Civil War as useless bloodshed. However, they also describe him as filled with "boundless kindness and benevolence towards mankind" (p. 200). In the Bardo, most of the spirits step into Lincoln's body and impart their experience to him, and when he leaves the graveyard, the spirit of a former slave remains in his body. Lincoln seems to empathise through this experience and resolves to continue the Civil War in order to provide equal opportunity throughout the country.

MANDERS

Manders is the graveyard's night-watchman who ushers Lincoln to his horse and back. He is the only other 'living' character besides Lincoln present for the action of the novel.

ANALYSIS

THE BARDO, SICK-BOXES, AND MATTERLIGHTBLOOMING PHENOMENON

Saunders places much of the novel's action in the Bardo, a term derived from the Tibetan Buddhist word for the transitional state between one life and the next. In this philosophy, the bardo is the space wherein the soul is disconnected from the body after death, and it can provide either the opportunity for deeper spiritual knowledge (sometimes transcendence) or nightmarish hallucinations borne of bad karma from their previous life.

Saunders' novel, indeed, takes place in an in-between state that is never in the text specifically identified as either a bardo or a more Christian conception of purgatory. The characters instead refer to themselves as sick and to their coffins as sick-boxes. When Willie first catches sight of his body in the coffin, he is unable to recognise himself, instead describing it as, "the Worm the size of a boy" (p. 34), and, indeed, the spirits in the graveyard refrain from accepting that they are dead for fear of the matterlightblooming phenomenon. Through this use of language, Saunders makes the world of this in-between state and the idea of what comes after passing on as unknowable and unfamiliar to the reader as it is for the characters. Indeed, it is Willie's utterance of the word 'dead' that precipitates the passing on of the majority of the graveyard, suggesting that is the confrontation of a uniting principle of being (or, in this case, non-being) that allows each character to move on.

Imagistically, Saunders metaphorises the themes of regret and longing for more that ostensibly keep the spirits in this in-between state. For example, the character of Jane Ellis, who in life hoped for an independent existence filled with travel but instead succumbed to marriage and placed all of her hopes in her three daughters, is plagued in the Bardo by three orbs that resemble her daughters and that perpetually crush her under their weight. Similarly, Mrs. Abigail Blass, frugal in life, spends her existence in the Bardo bent towards the ground, and Mrs. Francis Hodge, a slave, has bloody stumps in the Bardo where her hands and feet used to be. After the spirits have inhabited one another, however, these exaggerated features disappear, and at the moment that they pass on, they leave their clothing behind in the Bardo; this suggests that, once understood fully by another, the characters are no longer literally crippled by the single aspect of their identity which others believed defined them in life. The shedding of these features and the clothing suggests that passing on and the matterlightblooming phenomenon is, indeed, the blooming or blossoming of new potentiality.

In their ability to inhabit both the bodies of the living and the spirits of one another, the spirits of the dead are able to commune not just with the thoughts of others, but with their knowledge of the past and present as well. After first doing so, Bevins remarks that "we were perhaps not so unlovable as we had come to believe" (p. 70), and Saunders explores this notion of empathy and community – particularly juxtaposed with the utter isolation of the cemetery, where families no longer visit the spirits – as that which provides the characters with the resolve to pass on. The knowledge of their goodness and their accomplishments in life is counterbalanced with the sentiment that "none were content   All had been wronged   Neglected   Over-looked   Misunderstood" (p. 82). Saunders ties this notion to Lincoln's final resolve, after having been inhabited all the spirits in the graveyard, including former slaves, that a human's capacity for suffering is that which ultimately connects them to all others.

POLYPHONY AND HISTORICAL FICTION

Lincoln in the Bardo is firstly and notably quite different from other novels in terms of its form. Structured as though made up of a series of first-person accounts, the novel interpolates both fictional passages from the voices of those in the Bardo and passages that provide historical accounts of Lincoln and the events preceding those in the novel. Saunders, however, intentionally includes *fictional* historical accounts, blurring the line between what is fact and what is fiction even further, creating a form-content relationship whereby the voices of the dead mingle with the voices of the 'living' in a kind of transitional space; the novel becomes, in effect, the Bardo, where the souls of the dead might be analysed for what they would have been in life in the same way, Saunders suggests, that all of history is essentially speculative.

Saunders uses counterpoint throughout, using historical accounts to both corroborate and confuse the action of the novel. For example, Bevins and Vollman disagree as to whether Lincoln is sobbing upon arrival at the graveyard (p. 44), just as the historical accounts depict contradictions between historical witnesses. "The terrible storm without seemed almost in unison with the storm of grief within" (p. 55), says one historical witness, creating a pathetic fallacy with Lincoln's grief and suggesting that truth is sometimes as strange as fiction. Most significantly, Saunders uses historical passages to break up Lincoln's train of thought, moving from the speculative to the historical in order to both provide the reader with an understanding of Lincoln's conflict pertaining specifically to the

Civil War, and place the reader in Lincoln's shoes. In this way, the weight of Lincoln's thoughts is bolstered by a very literal sense of history, and the grandness of his endeavour is felt more deeply.

The reader is, in effect, brought back from the fictional world of the Bardo to a sense of 'reality' in the same way that Lincoln is brought back from mourning to remember the reality of the Civil War.

Moreover, this form creates a sort of democracy of voices that is at once dialogic – and, indeed, much of the novel reads rather like a play – and polyphonic, creating a form-content relationship whereby the reader is confronted and filled with a plurality of voices in the same way that Lincoln is finally filled with the voices of the spirits that fill his son's graveyard. This democracy of voices confirms the thematic exploration of Lincoln's motivation to continue the seemingly fruitless Civil War, and the novel itself becomes away for the voiceless to be liberated – to tell their story – in a way that Saunders suggests Lincoln hopes to provide for all in his country.

SLAVERY, DEMOCRACY, AND AMERICAN HISTORY

Most strikingly, Saunders uses his novel to investigate and speculate as to Lincoln's motivations, in spite of doomed forecasts for the outcome of the Civil War, to continue on with what eventually would become the course of history. In the novel, Lincoln is as much in a threshold or transitional state as the spirits in the graveyard, forced to choose between abandoning the war effort or continuing on in spite of the incredible causalities and – at the time of the novel – unsuccessful campaigns. "We were at war. We were not at war" (p. 174) thinks Lincoln, in a statement that neatly describes the cognitive dissonance and inherent threshold world of a Civil War – a country at war with itself.

Saunders therefore positions the voices of slaves at the forefront of the climax; when they inhabit Lincoln, they relate the brutal details of their treatment, prompting Lincoln to believe that suffering is that which unites all humans. By allowing the voices of slaves a voice in the novel, Saunders suggests that it is the ability to listen to another and to – quite literally – absorb their history and their narrative – that has the ability to affect the course of history. Indeed, Thomas Havens, in inhabiting Lincoln's body, says that "if not permitted to tell [one's story], one must think it and think it" (p. 255).

FURTHER REFLECTION

SOME QUESTIONS TO THINK ABOUT...

- Why does Saunders choose to place 'historical' passages throughout the fictional narrative? What expositional, thematic, or formal purpose do they serve? Does their purpose change as the novel progresses?
- Analyse the extreme physical features of each character in the Bardo. How does Saunders use this imagery in order to create character without the use of narrative exposition?
- Is the Reverend's account of 'the final judgment' to be believed? Why or why not? Will all characters encounter the same kind of judgment as the Reverend?
- Discuss Elise Traynor's fate and the carapace that develops around Willie. What is Saunders suggesting about the conflict between innocence and death?
- How would you describe Saunders' form? Epistolary? Theatrical? What does he gain by writing in a nonstandard narrative mode?

- How does the chorus of voices (or contributors) throughout the book inform the novel's themes of empathy, connectivity, and identity?
- Discuss Thomas Havens' final journey. Does Saunders suggest that Lincoln understood the pain of slavery in the literal or the abstract?

We want to hear from you!
Leave a comment on your online library
and share your favourite books on social media!

FURTHER READING

REFERENCE EDITION

- Saunders, G. (2017) *Lincoln in the Bardo*. London: Bloomsbury.

REFERENCE STUDIES

- Bowker, J. (2000) Bardo. *The Concise Oxford Dictionary of World Religions*. Oxford: Oxford University Press.

Although the editor makes every effort to
verify the accuracy of the information published,
BrightSummaries.com accepts no responsibility for
the content of this book.

www.brightsummaries.com

Ebook EAN: 9782808019323

Paperback EAN: 9782808019330

Legal Deposit: D/2019/12603/133

Cover: © Primento

Digital conception by Primento, the digital partner of
publishers.

Printed in Great Britain
by Amazon